AF334847

CHOP SHOP

Stephanie Taylor

with an Introduction by
Vanessa Place

TRENCHART: The Parapet Series

♪

LES FIGUES PRESS

Los Angeles

Designed and edited by Les Figues Press.
Printed and bound by Hignell Book Printing, Winnipeg, Canada.

Chop Shop
FIRST EDITION

ISBN 10: 0-934254-01-0
ISBN 13: 978-1-934254-01-1
Library of Congress Control Number: 2006938490

The TRENCHART Parapet series is made possible through the contributions of subscribing members. Les Figues Press thanks these members for their support and encouragement.

TRENCHART is a project of Les Figues Press, a nonprofit independent publisher of unconventional literary prose and poetics. TRENCHART titles are available in select independent bookstores and online at www.spdbooks.com. Each TRENCHART series is also available by subscription membership; becoming a member is the best way to ensure your complete collection of TRENCHART titles. For membership information, see Les Figues Press website at: www.lesfigues.com.

Publisher's Note: Special thanks to Jennifer Calkins, Danielle Adair, Maude Place and Fergus Place.

Distributed by SPD / Small Press Distribution
1341 Seventh Street
Berkeley, CA 94710
www.spdbooks.org

TrenchArt 3/4
Book 5 of 5 in the TRENCHART Parapet Series.

ƒ

LES FIGUES PRESS
Post Office Box 35628
Los Angeles, CA 90035
323.934.5898 / info@lesfigues.com
www.lesfigues.com

CHOP SHOP

Room Gallery, University of California, Irvine
organized by Juli Carson
January 19-February 10, 2006

Galerie Christian Nagel, Berlin
28 April-24 June 2006

Generali Foundation, Vienna
17 January-29 April 2007

This book is made possible with financial support from Galerie Christian Nagel and Daniel Hug Gallery.

Special thanks to: Juli Carson, University of California Irvine, Poor Man's Expression, Florian Zeyfang and Martin Ebner, Christian Nagel, Daniel Hug, Tony Fernandez and Dealer's Choice, Lincoln Tobier, Parisa Taghizadeh, Diana Watson and Native Tile, Wook Kim, Andy Alexander, Lars Friedrich, Susanne Prinz, Jeremy Higginbothon, Mike and Eli Holz, Vanessa Place and Teresa Carmody.

Contents

Introduction

Without words no objects without objects no words without the word as object without the object as word as the word is object is word. *Virevolter*—the thing turns on itself, and in the turning, turns. Stephanie Taylor's *Chop Shop* is the chronicle of an exhibition and the exhibition of a chronicle. It is a book. It is a demonstration. It is an aggregation that cannot exist other than it is, though as it is is entirely capable of transformation.

The process is simple and simultaneous. Like any ideal metamorphoses, the change of one thing into something else is startling and inevitable, and implicates an essential dissolve between container and contained. Man is an insect; woman, a soft-eyed heifer, or set of stems, to be played on by Pan. There is elemental order in such formal exchange: the external nature shrinks and extrudes, hairs up or pairs down, does whatever needs doing to fit the more natural internal nature. There's a sense of punishment, or at least just desserts—lovely turned lowly Io as much a temptress as she was tempting, and Gregor, bugging—as if the veil of the external's the only vestigial bit of goddishness humans have left. Taylor takes over the role of transformer, and refuses to allow any gap between natures: the skin is the flesh of the thing.

She begins with a text of some meaning, such as a song or poem, creating rhyme-charts of each word; the rhymes typically maintain vowel-sounds (the spirit of the thing), transposing primary consonants. From these rhyme-charts, Taylor makes another text, another song or poem that has some other meaning. From this text, she makes objects. The objects are created according to both the nature of the rhyme-text and the nature of the thing made. Word and object are inalienable and indivisible. A thug is made of a mug. Note, by the way, that a thug is often made by his mug, by way of identification, *i.e.*, the mug shot. Taylor's thugs' mugs are the kind that hold coffee, good for the get-up and go, *i.e.*, the getaway. Likewise, thieves are caught (or hidden) in leaves, as thieves would be caught hiding in the bushes or beating a hasty retreat. A rear-door is a mirror: in any looking back, we see only our reflection. Objects—a mug, a mirror—as incantory and contingent as language itself, existing first and last in the fact of their utterance—a mir-or image is a backward view of what we would see if we were able to twist round and see ourselves fully forward. Every word in Taylor's world is rendered concrete as concrete: it is not by accident that nothing's nature-made. There's no marble, no stones man-handled into submission. By making her fabrications out of the already-fabricated, Taylor affirms the correspondences between creations. Made-meaning and made-object are not in analogous or symbolic agreement, and never in coincidental agreement, for word is to object like a joint to its meat. The mug makes the thug made of the mug which makes the thug. The thing is the thing in all its rhyming reason.

Some people slap the nonsense label to Taylor's work, seeing only Seussean play in a can of gas made of brass. There is plenty of play, to be sure, but it's play on a strict phenomenological field, and true nonsense is never truly nonsensical. If there's one, as Bertrand Russell took pains to note, there's bound to be two, and if there's two, forty-six *will* certainly come forty-four later. And if playing-cards are to be your soldiers, then you may only have forty, for face-cards *will* expect to be waited upon, even Jacks. Of course, in Taylor's world, there's also the willing probability that two's to be to, and to be, too, and in these dueling to be's are borne new lattices of cabbaged meaning, by which I mean to say as centerless and ordered as the sea-green ocean. Navigable, but fairly teeming. To see then, with optricks:

As noted, everything is quite itself, and more. In this sense of exponential essence, Taylor embraces what Rosalind Krauss has called a new "medium-specificity" (Krauss, *A Voyage on the North Sea: Art in the Age of the Post-Medium Condition*), a polyglot aesthetic in which the properties of the medium include all the properties emanating from that medium. To nutshell: the modernists held painting as an exploration of the properties of paint, increasingly restricting its manifestation to this specific materiality, so that any decorative or representational element must be shucked, not just as an unnecessary distraction, but, like the shell of an oyster, a hindrance to the heart of the matter. This idea of medium as the quala of that medium is replaced in conceptual art by medium as "aggregative." All properties and materialities of the art-form become part of the medium, and generally-specific to that sort of medium: the act of painting is part of the fact of painting. The aggregative, in turn, generates a new set of conventions, some purely specific (paint), some purely experiential (painting), all wholly interrelated (the painting). Creating a continuum is created from a degenerate essentialism (the simple, single point of paint) to its mirror-twin, nondegenerate existentialism (the general and complex points of painting), resulting in a constellation, an infinity of points where there is no difference between subject and object, painting and painter, canvas and wall, wrist and color and light and socket and the sound of squeaking sneakers on the lemon-scented gallery floor. The new mediums [multiple]-specificity insists on a unity between surfaces and supports in which—like a pot of oyster stew—the object "is utterly coextensive with its own origins." (Krauss 53) But where modernist and conceptual art resists the narrative urge, Taylor embraces and compounds it. In *Chop Shop*, the origin-text is a song. Songs are in-themselves indivisible from their medium, for music lies only in music, a felt-sequence of circumstantial sound and silence, bookended as a moment of music by calling it a song. (Famously proved by Cage's *4'33"*.) Lyric is, by its particular properties, as naturally twinned to its music as snakes to a tree.

Hang on, there's the legerdemain, the bit of bright fluff and unsense that gives cardinal weight to Taylor's work—the "pseudo-sequence" identified in Elizabeth Sewell's 1952 book *The Field of Nonsense* as the adhesive of logical progression. Connective tissue that is just tissue, thin and see-through, but connective all the same because of the sinewed nature of our connections. The pseudo-series is most easily shown mathematically: as duly noted (and as unhinged to any particular reality), one surely predates two as three fronts four: saying something has forty-four applications, and not a single digit more, fixes that thing ontologically. Ontology, as anyone with a scrapbook or family photo can attest, is real as anybody's business. Similarly, rhyme schemes and alliteration are ordering devices of the first order, false and friend in equal measure, and in this, Taylor does a prefatory pirouette, taking the lyric of the origin-song (Woody Guthrie's "Take Me Riding in the Car"), with its own narrative logic ("front door, back door, clickety-clack"), and pricking out alternative rhymes ("take" = ache, bake, brake, cake, drake, fake, etc.); the alternative rhymes produce an alternative narrative ("For the sake of the spree"), with its own narrative logic ("filing quickly past the pack"), including an alternative musical number ("Chop Shop")—the sequence becoming an $n+1$, or $n^n+33\frac{1}{3}$. There's no stopping these generative geometries once they go into play, because the truth is that one does follow two in what we agree is reality, and "clickety-clack" runs as trippingly from the tongue as "past the pack," and both once uttered, feel utterly real. As Taylor takes these tissues and turns them tensile, then reality is rendered most real. And as furtively beautiful as a cartoon.

I originally thought of Taylor's work as an inverted, loopy ekphrasis: the visual becomes a poetic text which becomes another visual. But I think that's too cul de sac, for the work's more screely than that. Each rhyme made reason implicates other rhymes, equally reasonable. This manifold rationality suggests at once the way we choose to frame our exteriorities (by way of story or other cogitate association), and the way that framing is neither inherently inherent nor inherently arbitrary. We like things that seem the same to be set side-by-side: human disinclination/distaste for random mating is evident in everything from museum curatorial preferences to adjustment of the Hardy-Weinberg equilibrium in DNA analysis. While we will allow that some of this sameishness may be personal, if not idiosyncratic (toast *with* butter, please), some is not (toast = *Prosit!*), and some is really not (the mucous-lined need for food and hope). By this same token, Taylor is not Oulipean: although her work is constraint-based (though in this, the knobbed-throat set might insist hers is more "technique" than true constraint), it insists on internal meaning (though in this, its sensibility lies closer to Georges Perec and his moot and muted *eux* than current constraints' more moribund and mannish machinations). Sound is sense of some significance. Too, the work insists not just on individual or cultural meaning (though in this, there's that, as each rhyme-chart does not claim to be exhaustive), but rather the most gated meaning—that words are.

Therefore textual lines thrown are thrown forward across consciousness, read as red. For example, Taylor notes the January 2006 exhibit of *Chop Shop* ran in the "Vroom/Room Gallery" at University of California, Irvine.∴.

Now in this room there was a lusty rusty busty in full titular view, this voom-va-va-voom makes a gal leery, like the peek-a-boo of a cutie museum nudie. Still, she has the gall to leer at the gal on the go, the *va-va* which would be the ooh-la-la version of go-go, ergo, we're the Go-Go-Girls, as in vroom-vroom, as in *warum-warum*, the why-why? posited by our German allies, they who rush in and wonder as in mir-or, which is the view from the back, the rear door via which we all eventually exit, *fin* as a dying Cadillac.

For all her permutated play, Taylor constantly reminds us of the indefatigable fact *of*, that life is prepositional, that realism will poke its hairy knob through all our best efforts at abstraction, whether by the poetic redness of Rothko's rednesses or the undeniable sweetness of Toasted Susie's ice cream. So that evermore and back again, a song of true joy is a song of pure feeling. Because in this real and Taylor-made world, there is no object til the word, no word til the object, because the creator is us and we are our best and only eye-witness, so *virevolter*—

"—and it really *was* a kitten, after all." (Carroll, Through the Looking-Glass, chp. XI.)

Vanessa Place
November 2006
Los Angeles

Stephanie Taylor

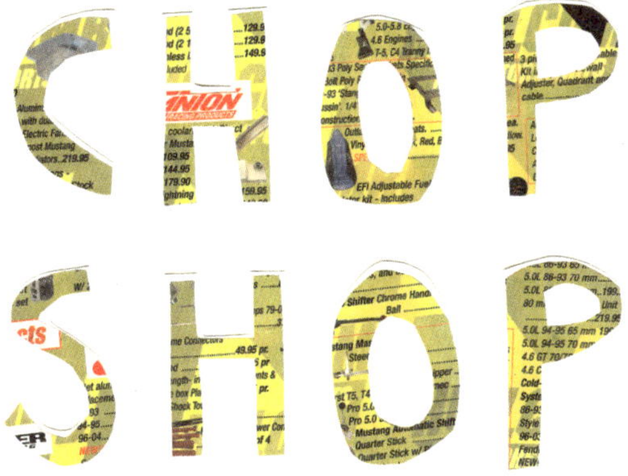

Chop Shop is the story of an oddly-dressed, shrub-ducking car thief who runs a phony tow-truck business in order to acquire parts for reconstruction and resale.

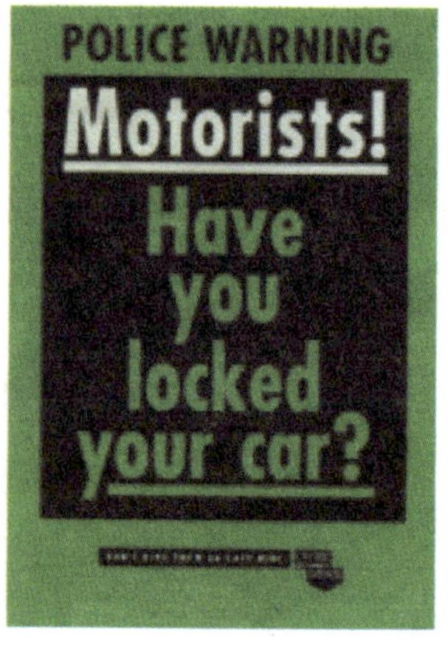
POLICE WARNING
Motorists!
Have
you
locked
your car?

CHOP SHOP
sound, 3:12 minutes

Stephanie Taylor and Dealer's Choice
sung by Woody Aplanalp

A	1
E	2
I	3
O	4
U	5

Chop Shop

For the sake of the spree bring a scarless skin.
4   \ | 5 (2   3 | | 2   3

A blooming few, filing quickly past the pack,
| 5   3   5   33   32 | | |

going then– hurling buoys– to the hunt.
4 3   2   5 3   52   5 | 5

(chorus)

A ton to tend and comb
| 5   4   2 | 4

then whole to set till morn.
2   4   5   2   3   4

Writ of crime: coning, cheating skulls.
3   5   3   4 3   2   3   5

like bad burning strep, erring parts, pens frozing numb.
3 | 5 3   2 | 3 | 2   4   3   5

Fleas, louses, hawk prongs clucking.
2   4 | 4   5   3

Tarred scags planning trips in boats.
| | | 3   3   3   4

(chorus)

Run rend the stolen chrome, men! ▃▃▃▃▃▃▃ *e*
5   2 | 42   4   2

Breaks, three sides– the thing is tin…and charred.
| 2   3 | 3   33 | |

The fumes flew miles.   *Flumes*
| 5   2   3

Ajar, dragging the fan strips the coats.
| | | 3 | | 3 | 4

(chorus)

Smart were the hens who chose to hum.
1   5   1   2   5   4   5   5

"Seize the grouse," says the strong squawking duck.
2   1   4   1   1   4   1   3   5

Nicked jacks towed, sworing earls.
3   1   4   4 3   5

Ploys blunt and grit slime spatting
4   5   1   3   3   1 3

that lulls pawns and beats the sylest cad.
1   5   1   1   2   1   3 2   1

[chorus]

Riding in my Car

Brrrm brm brm brm brm brm brm, brrrm b' brrrm,
Brrrm brm brm brm brm brm brrrm b' brrrm,
Brrrm brm brm brm brm brm brrrm b' brrrm.
Brrrm brm brm brm brm brm brrrm.

Take me riding in the car, car; (2x)
Take you riding in the car, car;
I'll take you riding in my car.

Click clack, open up the door, girls;
Click clack, open up the door, boys;
Front door, back door, clickety clack,
Take you riding in my car.

Climb, climb, rattle on the front seat;
Spree I spraddle on the backseat;
Turn my key, step on my starter,
Take you riding in my car.

Engine it goes boom, boom; (2x)
Front seat, backseat, boys and girls,
Take you riding in my car.

Trees and the houses walk along; (2x)
Truck and a car and a garbage can,
Take you riding in my car.

Ships and the little boats chug along; (2x)
Boom buhbuh boom boom boom buh boom,
Take you riding in my car.

I'm a gonna send you home again; (2x)
Boom, boom, buhbuh boom, rolling home,
Take you riding in my car.

I'm a-gonna let you blow the horn; (2x)
A oorah, a oorah, a oogah, oogah,
I'll take you riding in my car.

CHOP SHOP source text
Lyrics by Woody Guthrie

②

Take	me	riding		in	the	car	car	Take	you	riding		in	the	car	car	I'll
āk	ē	īo	ēng	in	a	är	/är	/āk	ū	īo	ēng	in	a	är	/är	/īl
ache	be	bide	bing	bin	∅	are	∅	∅	blue	∅	∅	∅	∅	∅	∅	aisle
bake	cree	chide	bring	been		bar		Brmm	brew							bile
brake	flee	cried	cling	chin		char		ŪM	cue							dial
~~break~~	fee	died	ding	din		czar		zoom	cluc							~~fite~~
cake	flea	dyed	fling	fin		dar		broom	crew							guile
drake	glee	dried	king	gin		mar		boom	due							mile
fake	key	eyed	ping	grin		par		bloom	dew							pile
flake	kney	guide	ring	flynn		mars		doom	~~few~~							rile
lake	lea	glide	sing	inn		par		flume	flew							stile
make	me	hide	sting	kin		r		fume	flue							smile
quake	plea	lied	sling	men		star		gloom	grew							~~sile~~
rake	pea	pried	spring	pin		~~scoot~~		loom	knew							trial
sake	sea	plied	string	sin		spar		plume	lieu							while
slake	see	ride	swing	shin		tsar		room	new							
snake	spee	side	~~thing~~	~~skin~~		tar		spume	rue							
steak	she		wing	span		yar										
stake	tea		wring	~~thin~~												

(marginal note by "lake": ride lea ends in me)

Spake
Shake
wake
owner
asleep

tree
thee
~~three~~ (circled)

slide
stride
snied
sighed
shied
spied
tide
~~tied's~~ (circled)
~~tried~~
vied
wide

zing

thin
twin
win
yin

tomb
whom
zoom

~~shoe~~ (circled)
~~spew~~
slew
~~screw~~ (circled)
true
through
two
too
view
who
you

wile

(3)

| click | clack | open the door | | | | girls | boys | front door | | back door | | clickity | | clack |
IK	AK	Ō	EN	a	ŌR	URLZ	ŌEZ	UNT	OR	AK	OR	IK	ITE	AK
brick chick click crick flick hick ~~kick~~ lick (nick) (pick) ~~quick~~ sick stick slick	back (black) crack flack (claque) (crack) hack (jack!) knack lack ~~back~~ (plaque) quack rack	bow blow crow dough doe floe fro ~~go~~ grow glow ho doe know lo low	glen hen ken men pen ten then when wren	∅	bore core chore drawer four fur floor ~~gore~~ hoar eoar more nore or poor pour roar (soar)	burls curls churls earl furr girt hurt pearls purl~? squirrels swirls twirls whorls whirls	~~buoys~~ joys noise poise ~~plays~~ toys	bunt brunt blunt ~~front~~ stunt grunt (hunt) punt runt shunt stunt	∅	∅	∅ ∅ a short letter or note	bit chit fit flit (grit) git hit fit knit lit nit pit quit	∅	∅

tick
trick
thick
wick

sack
shack
smack
stack
slack
snack
thwack
whack

mow
ho
oh
owe
pro
roe
row
sew
stow
slow
snow
toe
through
though
tow
to

shore
swore
store
score
spore
tore
war
yore

sit
skit
suit
split
spit
slit
shit
tit
twit
wit
whit
writ
zit

CLIMB   CLIMB RATTLE   ON   THE FRONT SEAT   SPREE ‡ SPRADDLE ON THE BACKSEAT   (4)

IM	ĪM	AT	UL	ON	A	UNT	ET	Ē	Ī	AD	UL	ON	A	AK	Ē	T
climesoto	∅	bat	cull	brawn	∅	∅	beet	∅	aye	bad	∅	∅	∅	∅	∅	∅
crime		brat	dull	con			beet		by	cad						
clims		cat	gull	dawn			bleat		bye	clad						
Clime		chat	null	drawn			cheat		cry	dad						
dime		fat	lull	don			cleat		dry	fad						
grime		frat	mull	fawn			eat		die	gad						
Irm		flat	scull	gone			feet		dye	grade						
LIME			skull	john			feat		eye	had						
MIME				pawn			fleet		fie	lad						
									fly							

(annotations: "crime", "LIME" and "gone" and "cheat" circled; "short fur and chat", "the loud", "of a" noted beside the AT/UL columns; "john – character name")

prime
rhyme
~~prime~~
slime
lime
thym

roaring 60 ice
nuder
slime

gat
gnat
hat
mat
pat
plat
sat
spat
splat
that
vat

on
Dawn
prawn
swan
spawn
wan
yawn
yum

greet
heat
meet
mete — to distribute as if by measure / a limit
meat
neat
pleat
sheet
skeet — a form of shooting birds
sleet
street
suite
sweat
treat teat wheat seat spy tie thigh

fry
guy
high
lie
lye
my
nigh
pie
pry
ply
tye
sky
spry
sign

mad
pad
plaid
sad
scad — a kind of fish or large # or amount
tad

sty shy tie thigh
thr thigh vr why wry

(5)

Turn my key / Step on my starter / engine it goes   um / um

URN	Ī	ē	ep	on	Ī	ärt	UR	en	in	it	ōz	um	um
burn	∅	∅	hep-hip	∅	∅	cart	burr	den	∅	∅	bows	chum	∅
churn			pep			chart	blur	hen			beaus	come	
*durn-dorn			prep			dart	cur	glen			crows	crumb	
ern-eagle			rep			heart	err	ken			chose	drum	
earn			step			mart	fir	men			close	dumb	
learn			shep			part	fur	flen			clothes	from	
			steep			smart	her	ten			doze	glum	
stern			schlep			start	myrrh	then			does	gum	
spurn			yep			tart	per				foes	hum	
tern							-				flows	mum	
urn							sir				froze	numb	
yearn							stir						

tern — "a bird / set of 3 / the lottery"
myrrh — aromatic gum resin

goes   plumb
grows   rum
glows   scum
nose   slum
knows   some
lows   strum
mows   swum
nose   thumb
ohs   gum
owes   bum
pose
prose
rose — color
rows
sons   sews   strows   scrows shows
Schmob   snows   toes tows   those throws rows

slur   when
spur   wren
were
whir

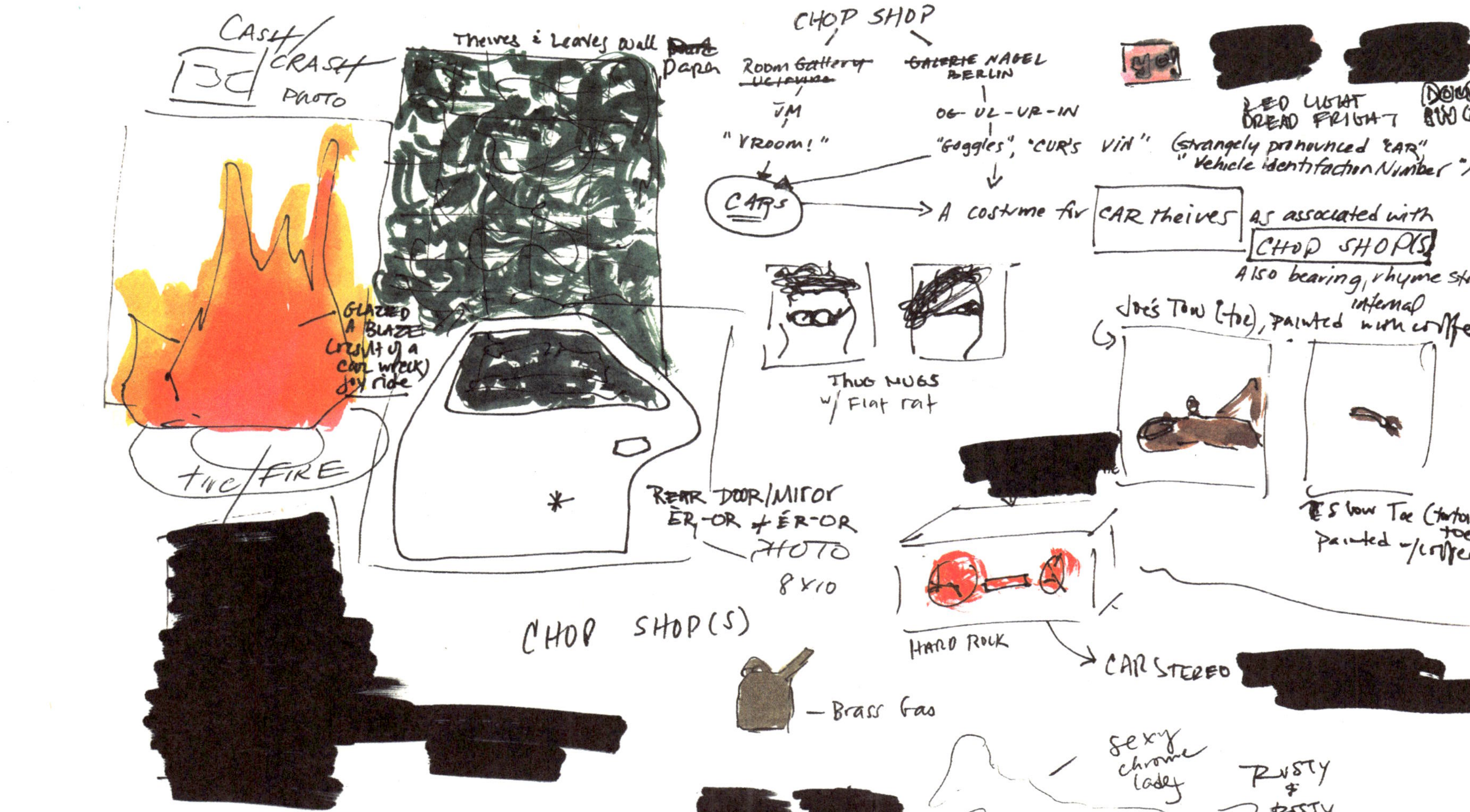

CASH / CRASH PHOTO
DC
Theives & Leaves Wall Papa
CHOP SHOP
Room Gallery Victoria
JM
Galerie Nagel Berlin
OG - UL - UR - IN
"VROOM!"
"Goggles", "CUR's VIN"   (strangely pronounced "CAR"
"Vehicle identification Number")
CARS
→ A costume for CAR theives as associated with
CHOP SHOPS
Also bearing, rhyme structure internal
LED LIGHT DREAD FRIGHT
DOUGH BUN CAFE
Thug MUGS w/ Flat rat
Joe's Tow (toe), painted with coffee
REAR DOOR/MIRROR ER-OR + ER-OR PHOTO
8x10
's low Toe (tortoise toe) painted w/coffee
GLAZED A BLAZE (result of a car wreck) joy ride
tire/FIRE
CHOP SHOP(S)
HARD ROCK
— Brass Gas
→ CAR STEREO
Sexy chrome lady
RUSTY & BUSTY

Trees and houses walk along truck and a car and a garbage can ⑥

ēz	and	ows	EZ	OLL/OK	ong	q-uk	and	a	ar	and a	ar	oSH	an
bees	∅	blouse	fez	ballk	gong	buck	∅	∅	ure	∅	∅	gosh	b an
breeze		(dause)	pez	caulk	long	chuck			var	(a jar)		posh	bran
cheese		grouse		chalk	prong	cluck			cher			smash	can
ease		louse	says	talk	song	duck			(far)			stash	clan
fees		mouse		block	strong	guck			star			hodge	(far)
flees		souse		chocks	tong	duck			man			podge	man
frees		spouse		chalk		luck			par			scag	pan
fleas		louses	sez	clock					star				plan
				crock					scar				van
				dawk									

notes: chickens to compl[ain]; a hallow in a surface or a depression

frieze
freeze
geez (from the mouth of a lout)
grease
fecs
koyp
knees
peas
pleas
peas
please
seize
tees
sprees
shes
sleeze

tease   teas   tweeze   thees   there   trees   threes   wheezes

dock
flock
frock
gawk
grok — to understand profoundly through intuition!
hawk
hock
jock
knock
lock
mock
pock
rock
smock
sock
stock

throng
wrong

shock   stalk

muck
pluck
ruck — a multitude / people who are followers
suck
stuck
shuck
struck
tuck

swalk   ralk

a crease
to crease

span
yare

drag

scan
span
tan
than
van

Ships and the little boats chuck along buh buh boom boom   ⑦

ips	and	a	it	ʊL	ōTZ	ʊk	a	oŋg	ʊh	ʊh	ūm	ūm
blips	∅	∅	∅	∅	boats	∅	∅	∅	∅	∅	∅	∅
chips					bloats							
clips					coats							
deps					dotes							
drips					floats							
flips					goats							
grips					gloats							
hips					mo ats							
lips					not es							
nips					oats							

quotes
knots
totes
throats
votes

grips
nips
pipes
skips
clips
strips
snips
tips
trips

⑧

I'm a-gonna send you home again rolling home I'm a gonna let you blow the horn

Īm	a	ʊn	a	end	ū	ōm	a	en	ōl	ēng	ōm	Īm	a	ʊn	a	et	ū	ō	a	orn
∅	∅	bun	∅	bend	∅	*(chrome)	∅	den	boll	the seed bearing capsule of certain plants	∅	∅	∅	∅	∅	bet	∅	∅	∅	born
		dun		blend		~~comb~~		glen	bowl							(dent)				corn
		done		end		dome		hen	cole							fret				~~dawn~~
		fun		fend		foam		ken	coal							get				mourn
		gun		friend		gnome		~~men~~	dole	kale						jet				sworn
		none		lend		~~home~~		pen	droll							met				~~slorn~~
		nun		mend		loam		ten	goal							net				shorn
		one		pend		pome		~~then~~	hole							pet				torn
		pun		penned		roam		when	knoll							set				thorn
		~~run~~		~~*rend~~ (to pull, split or divide)		~~tome~~		wren	(pole) — crash into telephone pole?							stet				worn
		Sun		Send				yen	roll							~~sweat~~				warn
		son		spend					role							(threat)				
		spun							stroll							vet				
		shun														wet				
		stun																		

get

soul
sole
shoal
* stole *
*
skoal ← used as drinking toast
scroll
toll
~~troll~~
whole

ton
tun
won

~~tend~~
brend
vend
wend

①

a	ooh	ra	a	oorah		a-oogha			a	oogah	
a	ū	a	~	ū	a	a	ū	a	a	ū	a
ø	ø	ø	ø	ø	ø	ø	ø	ø	ø	ø	ø

For the sake of the spree, ~~bring~~ bring a scarless skin.
A blooming few, filengquickly past (the pact) —stet
going then— soaring, hurling buoys— to the ~~hunt~~ hunt

writ of crime: skull's con^ning a ("cheat"), sigh.
Bad burning Strep, parts erring, pens frozing numb
Fleas, louses, hawks prongs clucking.
Tarred scags planning trips on boats. —(referring to a previous
crime ring on cruis ships.)

Run rend the chrome, men! "stolen"-threat and scorn.
Breaks, three sides — the thing is tin... and charred.

The fumes flew. miles.

Nicked Jacks towed, sworing earls.
Ploys blunt and gritty, slime spatting
that lull pawns and beat sly cads.

learn the step!
smart were the hens who chose to hum.
"Seize the grouse" says the squawking strong duck.

A jar dragging the far ~~stump~~ rips the coats
A ton to tend and comb
Then whole to set till morn.

CHOP SHOP: A Conversation between Stephanie Taylor and Juli Carson

Your project, *Chop Shop*, is an interdisciplinary, "site-specific" installation of sculpture, photography, and song. In this installation, as in past work, you begin with a pun based upon the look or sound of a word you've associated with the exhibition site, and you metonymically proceed from there. Can you describe the associative method of your working process?

The concept of site specificity has traditionally been important for artists making a connection between an artwork and an exhibition space, but subsequently it's become an overused term that means almost nothing. When something is emptied this way, it's an attractive starting point because there's space for redefinition. So I begin by making a ridiculously simple sound association, say with the name of a gallery such as "Room." In this case "Room" leads to the sound "Vroom" and the project becomes about cars. This is *site-specific* in the ludicrously empty way that this term is used colloquially. In its absurdity it's also a critique of language thrown around in art discourse.

But distinct from more ubiquitous site-specific projects, you work critically with the concept of genre. How does genre come into play here?

In my first exhibition, I used the sound of my name to develop the story. "Stephanie Taylor" sounds like "stay funny sailor," and so the story was about a sailor. The stories are developed in different ways each time I do an exhibition. But it's never the case that I say "I'm interested in cars…I'm going to make a show all about them." And yet the association isn't completely arbitrary. Cars are integral in Los Angeles, so they're obvious things to make art about. In fact, in this instance, cars play centrally as cover stories for my texts, which are written from pre-formed sound sequences, liberally edited, and made into song and objects derived from rhymes. The fact that so many artworks have been made about cars makes me indistinguishable among thieves, which of course is how thieves are happiest. The chosen genre is a self-imposed limitation. Each piece in the show must therefore have a sound-relation with its materials and also, in some more abstract way, tell the story of the car thieves. I try to work within the vernacular of a given genre, but I'm also always working within the vernacular of contemporary art.

Speaking of art vernacular, Eva Hesse was a prolific list-maker, constructing endless word plays and titles. Rosalind Krauss, in her book *The Optical Unconscious*, cites Hesse's intentions on the absurdity of word play, which I think relates to your project: "'My idea,' she had said in 1970, speaking about the aesthetics of composition, of form, 'is to counteract everything I've ever learned or been taught about those things, to find something else... If something is absurd, it's much more exaggerated, more absurd if it's repeated.'" This describes Hesse's tactic of repetition-as-absurdity. I bring this up because, while others have cited literary models for your work, they don't usually discuss what I'd like to call the sculptural-semiotic model evoked by Hesse. Does this model resonate with you?

I work in an additive process. Individual rhymes are based on the repetition of a sound. Sounds are limited in the number of things with which they rhyme. Each rhyme within a composition produces a portion of the narrative in that each work must be associated in some abstract way to car theft, even if this means I tell a story about someone who wears a rat's bed on her head and goggles. Things get ridiculous quickly when rhymes are compounded. The stranger the story, the more process is revealed.

With all this repetition, *contingency* seems to be, pardon the pun, the driving force. But it's not a force devoid of intellect or intention; in fact, your process is complexly semiotic.

Yes, there's always an element of surprise in what I am "able" to make within these self-imposed limitations. But sometimes it's the case that I decide I want to make something specific, and I simply find a material with a very elastic rhyme-relation to this thing. I allow myself all liberties when I need to change something to make it better. I sneak in phrases I find or write and have them pose as products of rhyme charts. The charts are more like a corrupt alibi than an art-making factory. Sometimes I have to stretch the boundaries of believability to make something work. For instance, in this exhibition, which is traveling to Galerie Nagel in Berlin, I introduced rhymes with mispronunciations. "Berlin" sonically breaks down as "ur/in," which becomes "cur" (car mispronounced) and "vin" (vehicle identification number). Normally "car" would require the syllable "ar" rather than "ur." The logic is that certainly somewhere there exists a place where "car" is pronounced "cur." This site, wherever it may be, is where the story takes place.

It's interesting how your brand of *absurdity-as-paradox*, which spins off visual/verbal puns, relates to the irrational act of lying out loud, another form of rational mimesis (or more corrupt alibi). It's what Lacan meant when he said "a too formal logical thinking introduces absurdities, even an antinomy of reason in the statement I am lying, whereas everyone knows that there is no such thing... If you say I am lying, you are telling the truth, and therefore you are not lying, and so on." So in a way, the surrealist-absurdist notion of "lying out loud" in order to hide relates to your work.

Yes. I can think of another example: the *Art & Language* painting "Portrait of V.I. Lenin in the style of Jackson Pollock." When the painting traveled to the Soviet Union for exhibition, in order to pass the border censors the artists retitled it "Portrait of a Man in Disguise." By announcing in the title that it was "disguised," it was able to pass through the censors because I think it was assumed that someone trying to disguise something wouldn't scream and yell about that thing being in disguise.

No, it's counter-intuitive...

I like making objects that are simple rhymes with material names. Viewers tend not to read visual art as a series of sounds. In this sense, the objects I make are made to be misread. The rhyme charts appear to be so systematic, and yet the stories that are produced are often so bizarre. But I don't see it as lying—often it's the case that things are not what they seem. It is necessary to make a story in the absence of comprehension. And it is not uncommon at a later date to marvel at one's wildly inaccurate estimations. In relation to first impressions, everything is in disguise.

On a local note, making car sculpture or work in L.A. always seems to be, in part, about Charlie Ray's work. It's interesting, though, that you openly "steal" from a source that has less to do with your work logically than, say, the *Art & Language* piece.

The drawing in the anti- theft silkscreen sketch *is* reminiscent of Ray's *Unpainted Sculpture*. It's a diagram that I found on the internet which is labeled with all the devices that can be added to a car to make it "theft-proof." What's funny is that the sketch has been sitting on my desk unresolved for some time now. I think it might be unusable in that it's not made of units which can be separated. So the anti-theft car is really what it is—a dead end for car thieves (like me). But *Unpainted Sculpture*, in a way, relates to my project only on the most superficial level since it's not a show that's been inspired by art about cars, and I have no particular interest in cars.

What about this connection between car theft and art theft? What do you mean by mobilizing this cultural metaphor?

Work that motivates me tends to have this divide between what is apparent and what is not immediately given. For instance, when one reads the absolutely dense descriptive scenes in a Roussel novel, it is unbelievable to imagine the stories are based on internal rhymes. This idea of taking something and making it unrecognizable is mirrored in the structure of the exhibition, in that all the texts are written with rhyme charts and all the objects are made with rhymes that are not visually present in the show. One sees objects that may seem to have something to do with cars. The source is hidden in the same way a car thief might paint a stolen part and disguise it in a new context hoping to sell it without going to jail. We are always and only working with parts, thus as artists we are criminals because we have to steal.

Can you describe some of the work more specifically in these terms?

Yes. For instance, the song playing on the car stereo installed in a carpeted box is a rewrite of the Woody Guthrie song "Take Me Riding in the Car." There's no way anyone would ever know this since every single word has been dissected and re-rhymed. This is my sense of humor, to take a simple song about riding in a car and completely rework it, but to keep the story essentially the same. It's still a song about riding in a car, only it's thieves who are riding. The melody of the rewritten song is composed of five notes which are based on the vowel sequence of the rewritten text. The music is a bit "hard" since it's for car thieves.

There's also a photo of a mirror in the shape of a car door. If you emphasize the first syllable of mirror so that it sounds like "ear" and the last syllable so that it sounds like "oar," together they rhyme with "rear" and "door." But this of course isn't what someone is going to think when they see it. And there's wallpaper composed of silhouettes amidst an intricate pattern of leaves. They're thieves in leaves, hiding and waiting to steal your car. There's also a sexy chrome lady hanging on the wall like one you might see on a truck bumper. But it's rusty. The title of the piece is "Busty," so it both rhymes with its exterior description and fits within the loose narrative of automobile culture. Each work has a description packed with rhymes, but for the duration of the exhibition they are pawns of an auto-theft gang.

Perhaps we should stop there, so we can leave some of the work 'hiding in plain view.'

"LOCK   it!"

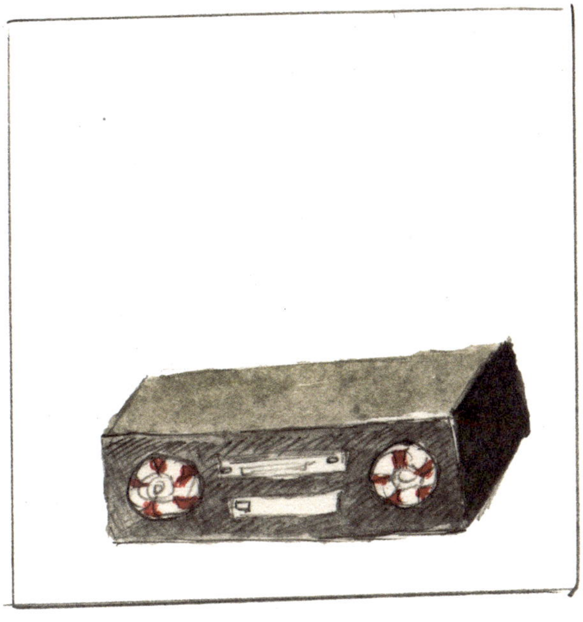

"Rock   it!"

MUSIC
+
AUTO tHEFT
= CAR STEREO + HARD ROCK

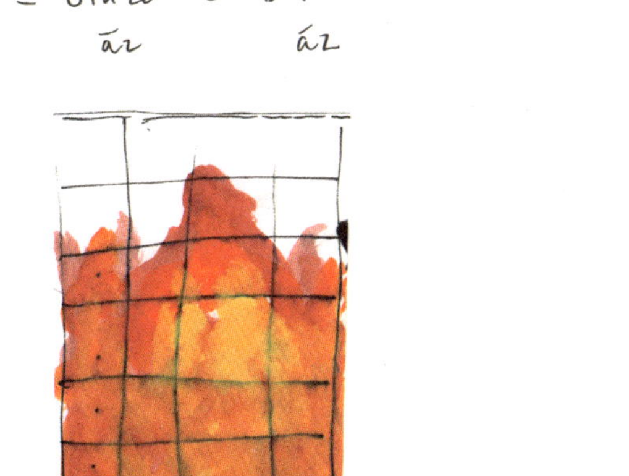

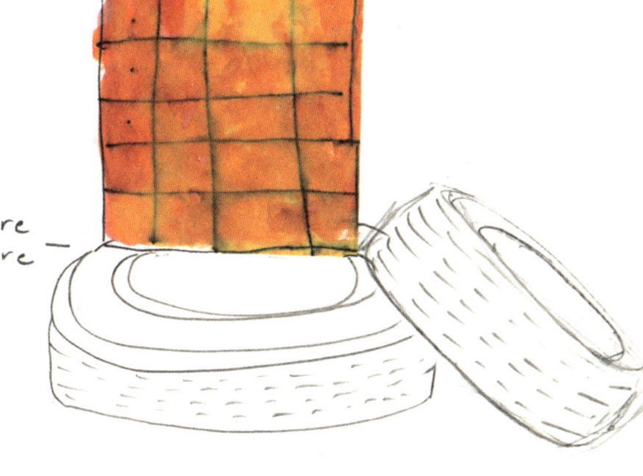

RESULT OF A JOYRIDE

DOUGH - "YO"
ō - ō
— PHOTO —

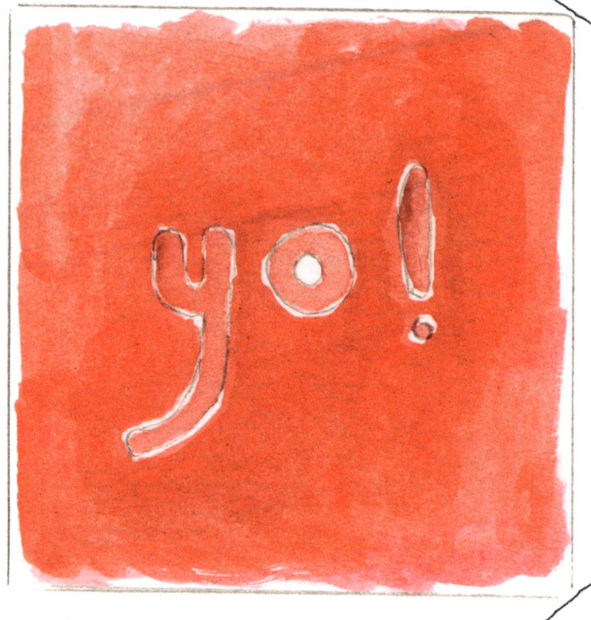

DARK PORTRAIT OF AUTO THEFT

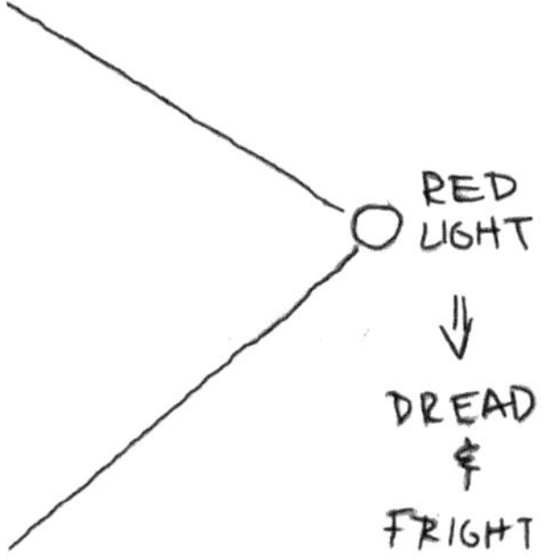
RED
LIGHT

DREAD
&
FRIGHT

— CASH   CRASH —
ASH — ASH

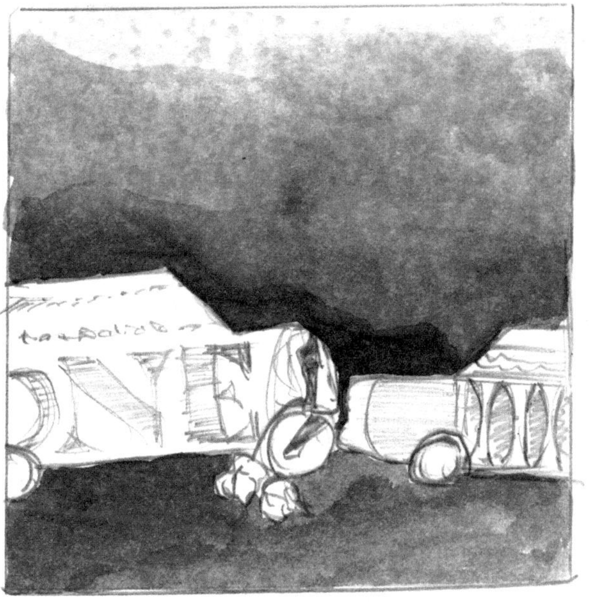

"ONE   IS   DONE

FIVE   IS   ALIVE"

FEMALE CRIMINAL
↓
DEVIL LADY

(FINE + SEXY LADY)

— RUSTY —
VST-ē

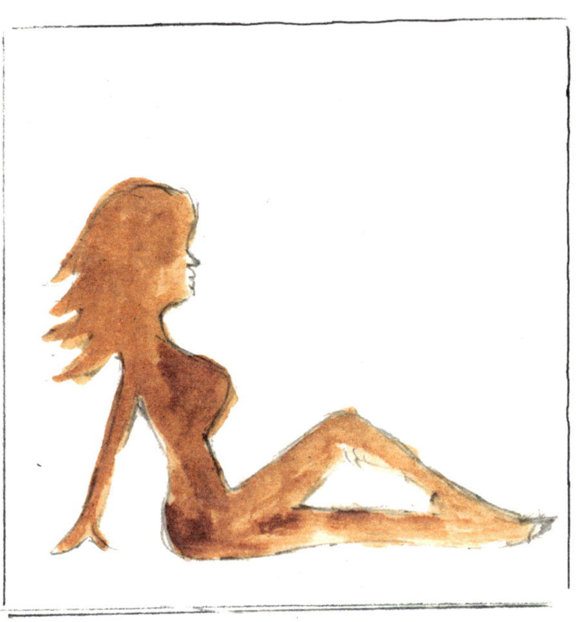

— BUSTY —
VST-ē

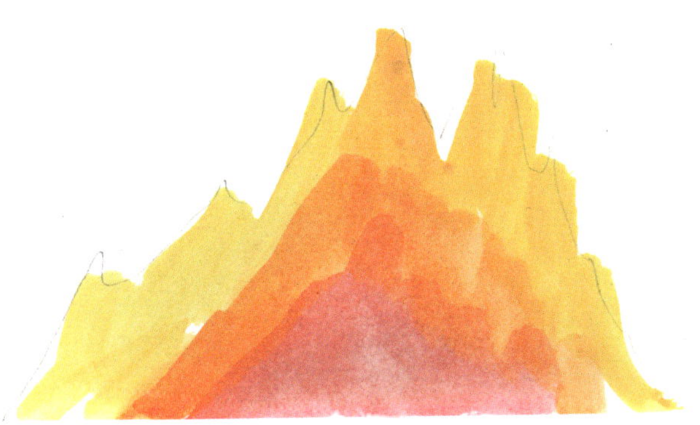

- REAR   DOOR -
ER   -   OR

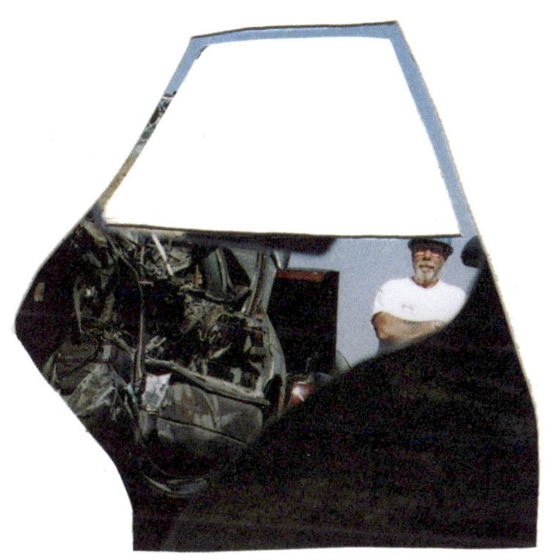

ER   -   OR

MIR - ROR

- MIRROR -

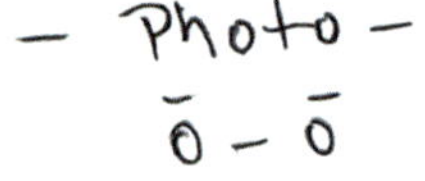

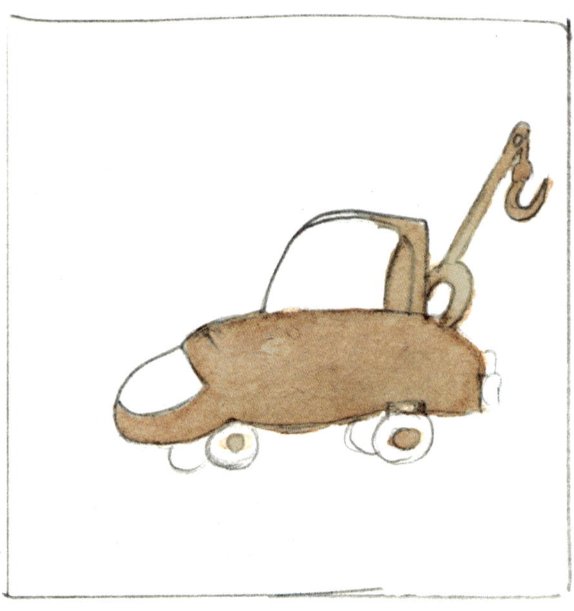

"Joe's Tow"

A toe, a ton   Vows

PAINTED
WITH
JOE
(COFFEE)

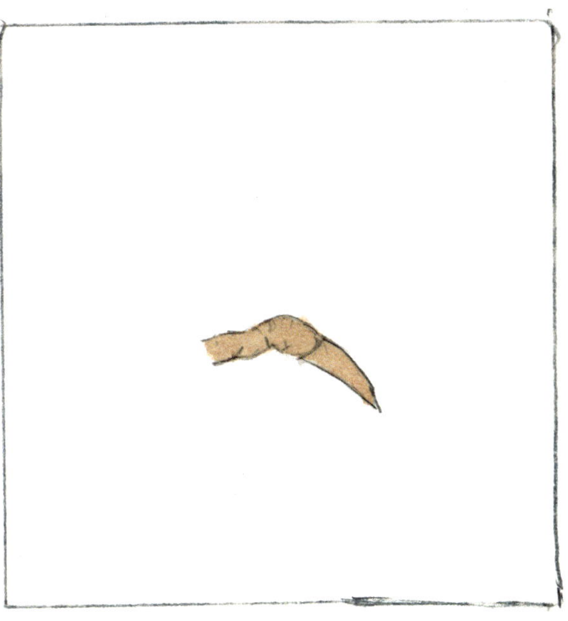

"SLOW TOW"

Quintessential slow toe =
tortoise toe

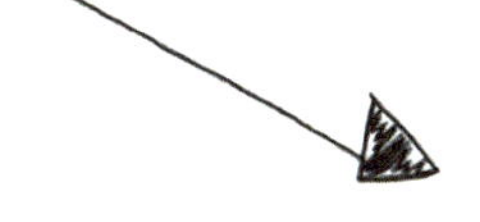

"Never a tortoise toe!"

THIEVES   IN   LEAVES

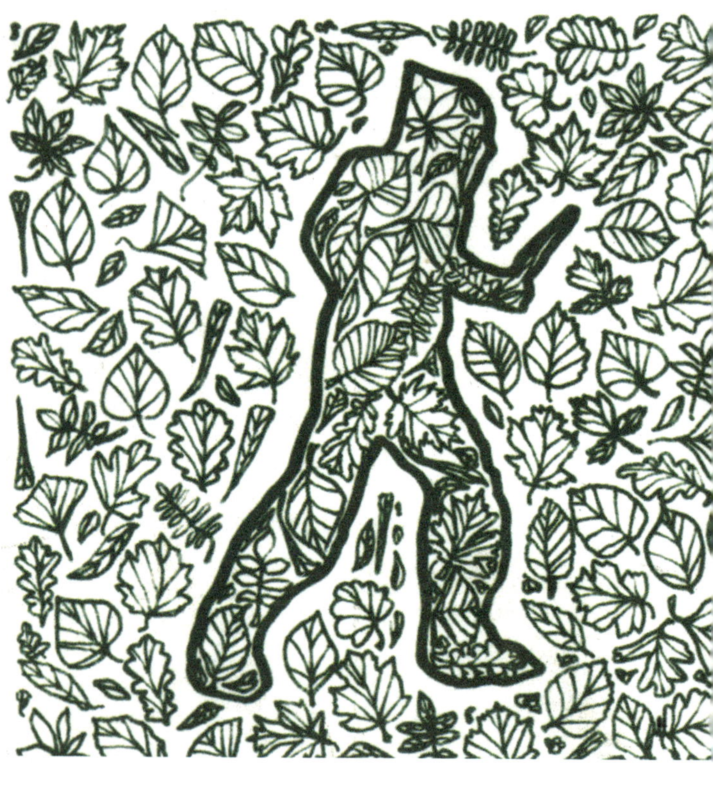

HAULING   CAPER
  ↓   ↓   ↓
AWL-ENG   ĀP-UR
  ↓   ↓   ↓
WALL   ∅   PAPER

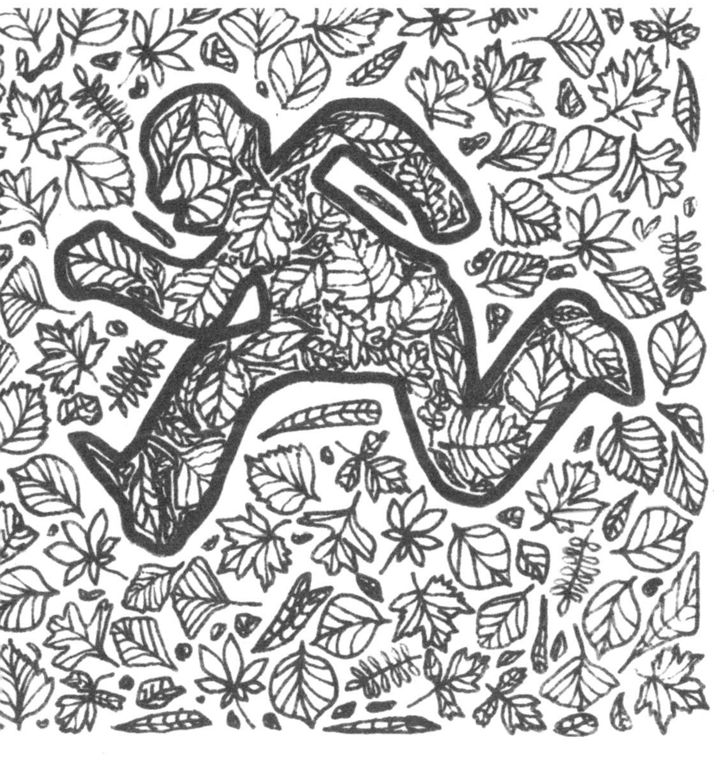

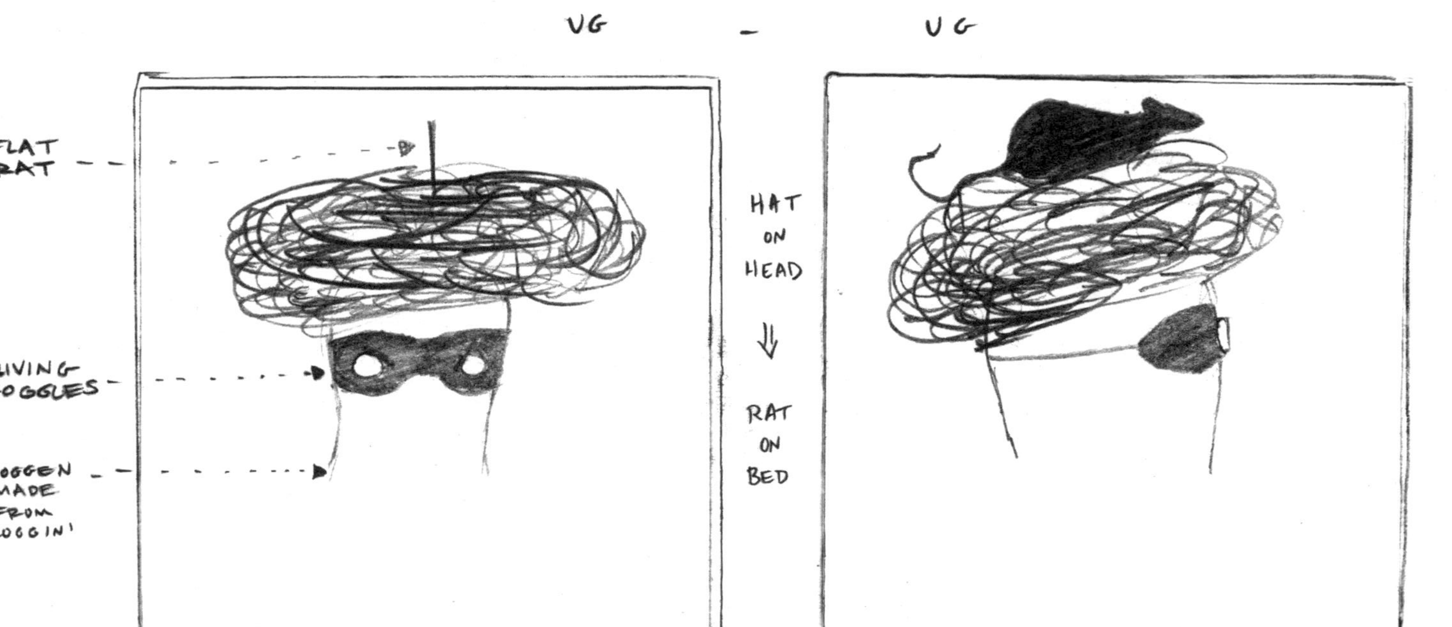
— MVG OF THVG —
VG — VG
FLAT RAT
DRIVING GOGGLES
NOGGEN MADE FROM LOGGIN'
HAT ON HEAD
RAT ON BED

Room (Gallery) → "vroom" / Nagel Berlin → GOGGLES, Cur - vin
COSTUME
(Exhibition in microcosm)
CAR
VEHICLE IDENTIFICATION NUMBER

BRASS

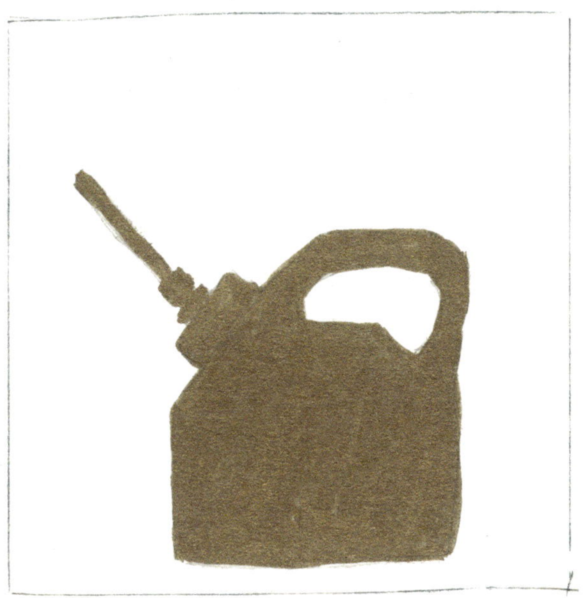

GAS

LURING WITH THE
PROMISE OF HELP

CHOP SHOP – ODER WIE KOMMEN DIE DIEBE IN DEN WALD

Die Arbeit Stephanie Taylors umfasst beinahe alle Kategorien künstlerischer Ausdrucksmöglichkeit. Ihr Repertoire reicht vom Scherenschnitt, über die klassische Metallskulptur bis hin zu Fotogrammen, Zeichnungen, Performances, Lesungen und Musikstücken. Diese formale Vielfalt halten Erzählungen zusammen, deren Handlungsstränge sich in linguistischen Verformungen und überraschenden Sprachvolten zu verlieren scheinen, um dann doch zum Handlungskern zurück zu kehren. Ausgehend vom nahe Liegenden, dem eigenen Namen, entwickelte Stephanie Taylor erstmals 2002 zunächst in freier Assoziation (Stephanie Taylor = Stay Funny Sailor) die Figur des Seemanns Anisar Condor, der an einer fiktiven Seeschlacht auf dem Mittelmeer teilnimmt. Von diesem Handlungsort leitete sich der Titel der Audioinstallation „Adria" ab, die eine Art Filmmusik zur Erzählung darstellt.

Dieser formbestimmende anagrammatischer Umgang mit Sprache sieht sich in konsequenter Nachfolge Ferdinand de Saussures und dessen Sprachtheorie, die u.a. den Signifikanten in keinerlei zwingenden Zusammenhang mit dem zugehörigen Signifikat sieht. So begreift Stephanie Taylor sprachliche Zeichen als lautmateriale Einheiten, mit denen Bedeutungen assoziiert sind, die durch minimale phonetische oder kontextuelle Verschiebungen variieren können. Das funktioniert deshalb so erfolgreich, weil Form und Inhalt bestimmter Wörter immer nur insofern eine spezifische Bedeutung zugesprochen werden kann, als die Kommunizierenden sie üblicherweise gemeinsam mit anderen sprachlichen Formen im Zuge der *parole* zu allseitig verstehbaren sprachlichen Ausdrücken zusammensetzen. Wenn aber nur ein einziger der Beteiligten aus dem etablierten Modus ausschert und sich in dadaistischer Manier der Sprache nicht als tradierten Gebrauchsgegenstand, sondern als Quell wunderbarer, originärer Laute nähert, denen es Leben einzuhauchen gilt, dann kann etwas ganz und gar

Eigenartiges geschehen: Die Sprache bildet keine Gedanken oder Geschichten mehr ab, sie erschafft sie vielmehr neu.

Obwohl das ganz einfach klingt, sind die so entstehenden Vokalextraktionen und Silbenvereinzelungen, Neuarrangements und Übersetzungen im Falle Stephanie Taylors verwirrend. Weil sie den Prozess der Artikulation zergliedert und an einer eher zufälligen Stelle im Strom der Gedanken eine höchst ungewöhnliche Abzweigung wählt, isolieren sich die Ausdrücke in ihren komplexen Erzählungen als Ausdrücke zunächst nicht identifizierbarer Gedanken, auf die dann sprachlich und bildlich Bezug genommen wird. Das geschieht natürlich in Taylors Muttersprache, dem Amerikanischen. An dieser Stelle fällt das Prinzip wieder auf sich selbst zurück, denn dass verschiedene Sprachen verschiedene Zeichen für - vermutlich – gleiche Bedeutungen verwenden – wie Saussure argumentiert – sich also die Bedeutung von Zeichen mit der benutzten Sprache verändern, ist eigentlich ein Beleg für das Taylorsche Arbitraritätsprinzip, denn es erlaubt quasi die freie Wahl eines Zeichens zu jedem erdenklichen Zweck. Gleichzeitig verhindert es aber die langsame Rekonstruktion des Gedankens beim Nachsprechen der Texte, weil sich schon der Titel der Ausstellung nur für den mit amerikanischer Umgangssprache Vertrauten erschließt. Einige Bedeutungsebenen von Taylors phonetischen, typografischen und akustischen Geschichten kann man letztlich wohl nur in ihrer Ausgangssprache vollständig ausloten.

Das ist nicht so erbaulich, macht aber letztlich auch nicht viel, gibt es doch nonverbale Ansätze zur Genüge. Das experimentierfreudig Hybrid aus Bild- und Textinformation in CHOP SHOP (2006) nahm beispielsweise seinen Ausgang in der eigentlich unbedeutenden Tatsache, dass es erstmals in der vermutlich absichtlich neutral genannten Room Gallery in der Universität von Kalifornien in Irvine gezeigt wurde. Der rote Faden dieser raumgreifenden Mixed Media Installation besteht aus Geschichten über Autos und Autodiebe. Von der Titel bestimmenden Skulptur *Chop Shop*, die wiederum außer aus einem Autoradio mit gleichnamigen Rocksong aus gefundenen Reimen in der Sprache präpotenter Autodiebe und zwei Gummireifen noch aus den Arbeiten *Tire Fire* und *Busty*, zwei weiteren Skulpturen aus glasierten Kacheln bzw der Silhouette eines großbusigen Pin-ups aus verrosteten Metall besteht, reicht das Repertoire bis zu kleinen verspielten Bilderrätseln und einer Tapete mit dem Titel *Thieves in Leaves*. Unwahrscheinlicher Beginn dieser Assemblage verschiedenster Gedankenvolten zum Thema Autodiebstahl lag in der zufälligen phonetischen Ähnlichkeit des im Amerikanischen gemeinhin für das Dröhnen eines Autoauspuffs verwendete „vroom" mit dem Wort „room". Der Ausgangspunkt einer weit mäandernden Bild-Geschichte war gefunden.

Mittels eines in seiner Komplexität absurden Vokalzählsystems auf der Basis eines Woody Guthrie Songs, das unter anderem aus unzähligen Reimkolonnen um Laute wie „ips", „ong" , „it" oder „um" kreist, die nach linguistischer Verwandtschaft sortiert, neu zusammengesetzt und mit einem flotter Rocksound unterlegt werden, von dem die Künstlerin annimmt „dass in Autodiebe auf Crashkurs" gerne hören würden, entwickelte Taylor eine Art Filmmusik, die ihre Geschichten akustisch begleitet. Der Ton macht quasi die Musik. Spielerisch illustrieren keine Fotoabzüge und Digitaldrucke die lose Reihung verschiedenster Anekdoten von Dieben und Rasern. Sieht man in *Rear Door* einen Dieb im Rückspiegel eines Autos, der praktischerweise gleich die ganze Innentür bedeckt, wird einem gleichnishaft in *Cash Crash* deutlich gemacht, wohin das alles führt, nämlich zu fatalen Unfällen, die Leben und Finanzen gleichermaßen bedrohen. Und natürlich trifft es die Armen auf den billigen Plätzen, denn *„one is done; five is alive"*. Wer daraus den Schluss zieht, dass grundsätzlich teure Autos beim Diebstahl vorzuziehen sind, dem sei *Mug of Thug* eine Mahnung. Dort sieht man die frontal und von der Seite die Visage eines Autodiebs – komplett mit cooler Sonnenbrille und einer Ratte auf der Matte. Diese wiederum hat gar nichts mit Autos zu tun, sondern sie ist im Fahndungsbild von Vorne eine lautmalerische *flat rat*, hat mithin also reichlich Daseinsberechtigung. Eher dem

Leben im Zwielicht der Illegalität gewidmet, dass das Dasein jedes echten Schurken bestimmt, ist die Tapete mit den Dieben im Schatten ihrer Blättermäntel. Diese *thieves in leaves* sind ein wunderbares Beispiel von Taylors raumgreifender, rein visuell orientierter Poetik. Jenseits aller klassisch strukturalistischen Klassifizierungskriterien sind sie – obwohl stark durch ihre kulturelle Herkunft geformt – durch ihre verhältnismäßig einfache Form allgemein verständlich. Über das unauflösbare Pardoxon, das es nun mal die Tücke im Umgang mit Text ist - auch in seiner materiellen Erscheinung -, dass man über ihn wieder nur mit Text schreiben kann, scheint Taylor nur zu spotten. Dieses Phänomen, das immer in seine Analyse hineingetragen wird, ist geradezu sine-qua-non ihrer Arbeiten. Während diesem (meinem) Text die Aufgabe zufällt, etwas, dem es formal bereits entspricht, mühsam zu erläutern, es mit der existierenden größeren Autorität des Bildes zu versöhnen, es ‚durchsichtig zu machen' in Hinblick auf das Zeichen, findet ihre Sprache ganz selbstverständlich zum Bild. Das „Coexistierende des Körpers" kommt bei Stephanie Taylor eben gerade nicht „mit dem Consecutiven der Rede in Collision" wie es in Lessings berühmter Vorrede zum Laokoon heißt. Vielmehr lebt es in fruchtbarer Symbiose mit ihr. Natürlich können wir seit dem Kubismus und Futurismus, dem Sprach zerstörerischen Dadaismus, dem Surrealismus, seit Schwitters Merzkunst und Marcel Duchamps Wortspielen in den Avantgarden eine wechselseitige Durchdringung von Text und bildender Kunst beobachten. Dieser Prozess besitzt aber gegenüber den tradierten Gattungsformulierungen in Literatur und bildender Kunst immer ein bestimmendes Charakteristikum: Kohärenz ist vollkommen unwichtig,

Susanne Prinz
November 2006
Berlin

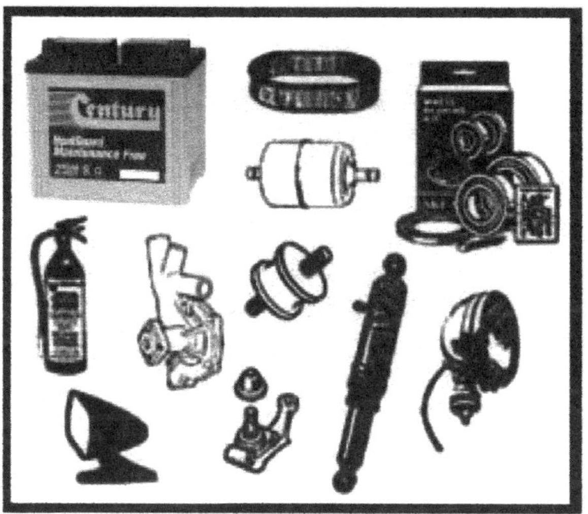

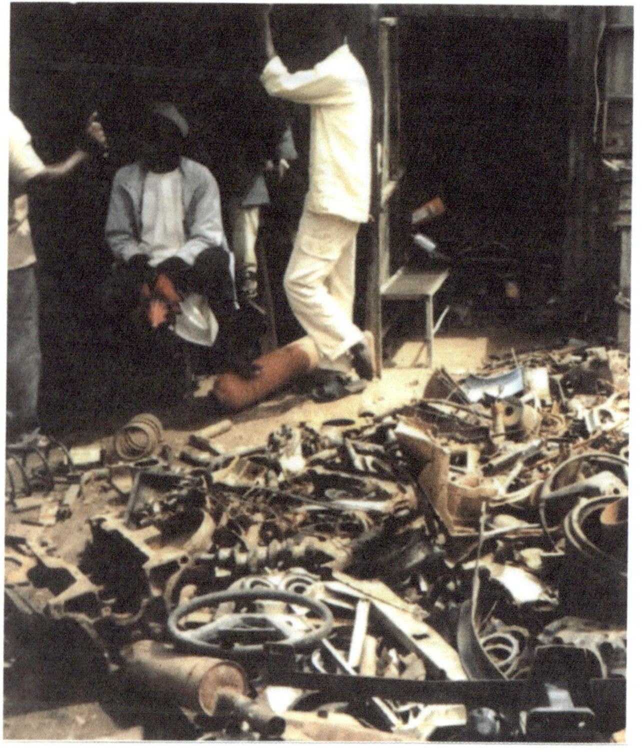

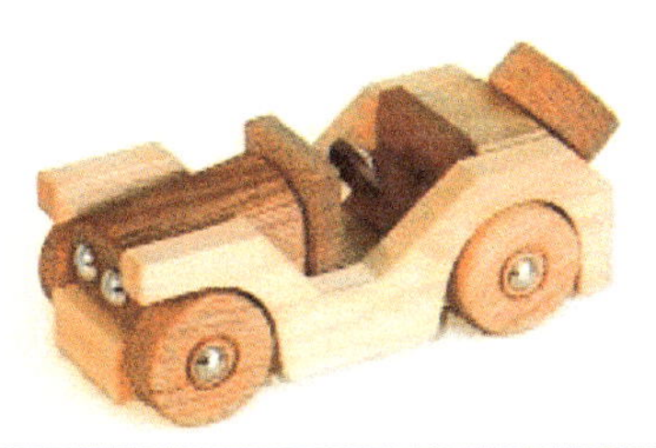

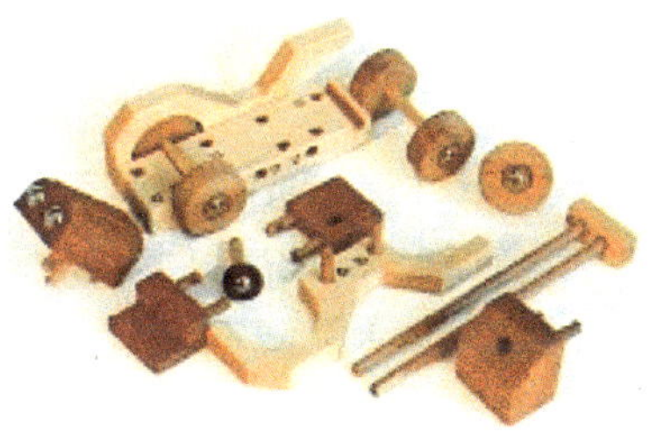

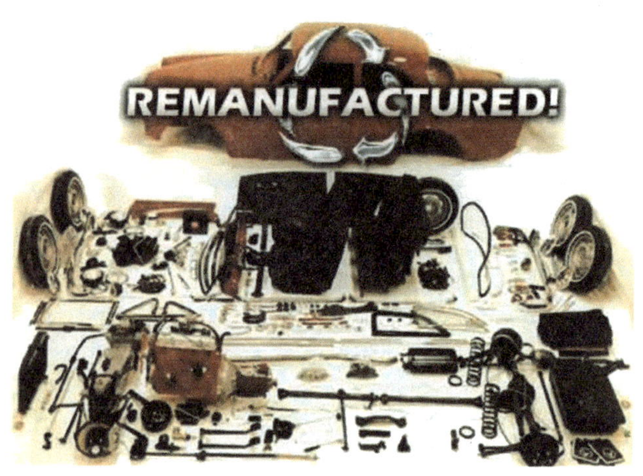
REMANUFACTURED!

PART

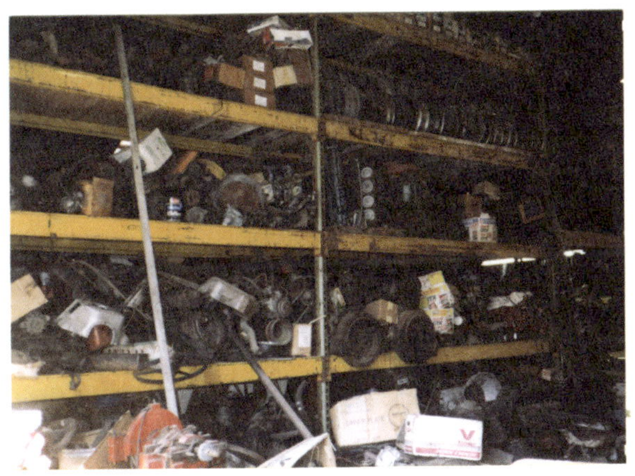

ART

Acknowledgements

CHOP SHOP: A Conversation between Stephanie Taylor and Juli Carson originally appeared in materials for the exhibition CHOP SHOP at Room Gallery, University of California, Irvine.

Back cover art by Danielle Adair, *White Matter*, stills from a video by that same name.

Image for "Part Art" from Michael Carmody's barn, #1.

Riding in My Car by Woody Guthrie. © 1954 (renewed 1982) TRO-Folkways Music Publishers Inc. NY, NY. United States copyright secured. Used by permission.

Stephanie Taylor received her M.F.A. from Art Center College of Design in Pasadena, California. She has exhibited her work internationally and is represented by Galerie Christian Nagel, Köln, Germany and by Daniel Hug Gallery, Los Angeles.

Vanessa Place is the author of *Dies: A Sentence* (2005), and a chapbook, *Figure from The Gates of Paradise* (Woodland Editions). Other work has appeared in various journals and anthologies, including *Northwest Review, Contemporary Literary Criticism, 4th Street, LA Weekly Literary Supplement, Five Fingers Review, Greetings #10/11,* and *The noulipian Analects.* Her nonfiction book about sex-offenders and the morality of guilt will be published by Other Press.

Danielle Adair is an M.F.A. candidate in Art and Writing at the California Institute of the Arts, Valencia, California. She uses video and performance in her visual art and is at work on her first novel.

Juli Carson is Assistant Professor of Studio Art, Art History, and Curatorial Studies at University of California, Irvine, where she is also Director of the University Art Gallery. She has just completed a book manuscript on conceptualism and psychoanalysis entitled *The Moebius Effect: Towards a Conceptual Unconscious in Contemporary Art.*

Susanne Prinz works as a freelance writer and curator, organizing exhibitions in France, Austria and throughout Germany. She curated *Portraits – A Tour Through 100 Years of Photography* for Getty Images, an exhibition shown in Hamburg, Munich and Vienna. Since 2002 she has served as director of the Galerie Christian Nagel, Berlin. She is currently the director of APT:Berlin.

LES FIGUES PRESS
PO Box 35628
Los Angeles, CA 90035
www.lesfigues.com

About the TRENCHART Series of New Literature

TRENCHART is an annual subscription series of innovative literature published by Les Figues Press. Each series includes four books situated within a larger discussion of contemporary aesthetics. The TRENCHART Parapet series also incorporates work by contemporary visual artists representing additional aesthetic explorations. By publishing individual titles as part of an annual series, the work is presented in conversation; to advance this exchange, all participants write an aesthetic essay or poetics, separately published as the series' leading title.

TRENCHART: Parapet Series

TrenchArt : Parapet
aesthetics
ISBN 13: 978-1-934254-02-9

Voice of Ice
Alta Ifland
ISBN 13: 978-1-934254-03-5

The Water Tower and Other Stories
Axel Thormählen
ISBN 13: 978-1-934254-04-2

God's Livestock Policy
Stan Apps
ISBN 13: 978-1-934254-04-2

Chop Shop
Stephanie Taylor
ISBN 13: 978-1-934254-01-1

Parapet visual art by Danielle Adair

Individual TRENCHART titles are available from Small Press Distribution (www.sbdbooks.org).

The complete TRENCHART Parapet series (5 books) is available from LFP for a Subscription Membership of $60 (US). For more information, see: www.lesfigues.com.

Published by Les Figues Press

TRENCHART: Material Series

Dies: A Sentence by Vanessa Place
Introduction by Susan McCabe
ISBN 13: 978-0-9766371-1-0

Grammar of the Cage by Pam Ore
Introduction by Ingrid Wendt
ISBN 13: 978-0-9766371-2-7

Requiem by Teresa Carmody
Introduction by David L. Ulin
ISBN 13: 978-0-9766371-3-4

A Story of Witchery by Jennifer Calkins
Introduction by Amy Gerstler
ISBN 13: 978-0-9766371-4-1

TRENCHART: Casements Series

in the plain turn of the body make a sentence:
Two Plays by Sissy Boyd
Introduction by Guy Zimmerman
ISBN 13: 978-0-9766371-7-2

INCH AEONS by Nuala Archer
Introduction by Pam Ore
ISBN 13: 978-0-9766371-6-5

Tribulations of a Westerner in the Western World
by Vincent Dachy
Introduction by Mary Burger
ISBN 13: 978-0-9766371-8-9

+|'me'S-pace, doc 001b.
from *For Love Alone, Christina'S-tead*
compiled by | Me
ISBN 13: 978-0-9766371-9-7

Other Titles by Les Figues Press

The noulipian Analects
edited by Matias Viegener and Christine Wertheim
ISBN 13: 978-1-934254-00-4

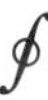

LES FIGUES PRESS
PO Box 35628
Los Angeles, CA 90035
www.lesfigues.com